Book 3
Egypt

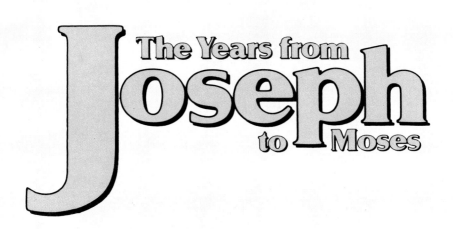

The Years from
Joseph
to Moses

Written by Anne de Graaf
Illustrated by José Pérez Montero

Adventure Story Bible

Bible Society

Egypt — The Years from Joseph to Moses

Contents — Genesis 41—end; Exodus 1—11

Book 3 — Bible Background

Joseph was made governor of Egypt, and ruled the country during the years in which there was not much food — the years of famine. He was also able to save his family from starvation, and be re-united with them.

Four hundred years later, a cruel Pharaoh made Joseph's descendants, the Israelites, into slaves. They had to work all day in the hot sun building pyramids and walls, and in the evenings they were given very little food. The Israelites could no longer look after their animals or enjoy time with their families.

Pharaoh was very happy having free slaves to do all the difficult and dirty work. But there was one thing that he had not taken into account.

The Israelites were God's chosen people. They knew that one day God would tell them to leave Egypt to return to the land which he had promised them so many years ago.

The Book of Exodus tells the story of how the people of Israel escaped from Egypt, led by a man called Moses.

FROM SLAVE TO PRIME MINISTER
Joseph Helps Pharaoh

Genesis 41.1-57

Joseph thought back over the past day.

He had woken up in prison and seen the usual pattern of sunshine and shadows through the barred windows of his cell, just as he had for the past two years.

Then there had been a lot of noise outside the prison. Pharaoh, the ruler of Egypt, had sent his guards and they were in a hurry. They rushed in. "Joseph," they said, "Pharaoh has heard how you understood the dreams of the cup bearer and the baker when they were in prison, and he wants you to explain a

dream that he has had. None of the wizards or magicians can explain it."

Joseph had been brought to Pharaoh, who had told him his dreams, and Joseph had just told Pharaoh what they meant — that there would be seven years of good crops and plenty of food, followed by seven years of famine — of bad crops when the food would run out, and people would be hungry.

"Now let Pharaoh put someone in charge of the food in Egypt. When there is plenty, the extra can be stored away and kept safe. When the crops fail, the people can eat the food in the storehouses and they will not go hungry," Joseph had said.

Pharaoh was now talking to his advisers about Joseph's advice. Joseph was standing some distance from them, wondering what would happen next.

The advisers stood back, and Pharaoh spoke.

"Your God seems to be with you in a very special way. He blesses you with the ability to see, where others are blind. I feel I can trust you.

"You shall be the man to do this task. It will be your job to rule my house, my people, and all the food stores in the land. There will be no one greater than you in all Egypt, except for myself."

Joseph staggered back a step. He could hardly believe what he heard. Pharaoh gave Joseph his own ring, a fine robe, and placed a gold chain around his neck. He also gave him the second royal chariot to ride in.

It happened just as Joseph said it would. During the seven years of good crops, Joseph made sure a fifth of all the grain was stored. He measured and weighed until there was so much grain, it could not be measured any more. He filled all the storehouses, then built new ones and filled those too.

When the seven bad years came, they were very hard and cruel. Egypt was the only country with food, and people from all over the world went there to find something to eat.

"There Is Grain In Egypt"

Genesis 42.1–4

The bad years, the years of famine, hit the land of Canaan, too. That was where Joseph's father and brothers lived. They had grown rich during the seven good years. Once the seven bad years started, however, Jacob and his eleven other sons used up all they had managed to save. Most of the sons were grown up and had families of their own to feed. So there were many mouths, but hardly anything with which to fill them.

The brothers grumbled among themselves. "What will we do now? Where will we find food?" they said.

Jacob knew there was food in Egypt. He had heard this from merchants travelling through the area. One day he said to his sons, "Why are you waiting here? If you don't want to starve to death, then go to Egypt. Take

money with you, and buy us some food."

The brothers loaded up their camels and donkeys and rode off towards Egypt. Not all of Jacob's sons left, however. Benjamin stayed at home.

Benjamin was about the same age that Joseph had been when his brothers sold him as a slave. Jacob had never got over the terrible loss of his favourite son, Joseph, but Benjamin had helped make the heavy grief a little lighter. Benjamin made his father laugh and smile. He learnt so quickly from Jacob, that it was always a challenge to come up with new things to teach him.

"No," Jacob thought, "I won't send Benjamin on a trip to Egypt. What would I do if I lost Rachel's second child as well as her first?"

Together Benjamin and Jacob waved and waved at the ten brothers, until all they could see was a cloud of dust and nothing more.

The Brothers Learn Their Lesson

Genesis 42.5–38

When the brothers arrived in Egypt they went straight to the man in charge of selling grain. That was Joseph. They did not recognize him because he was dressed like an Egyptian and spoke like an Egyptian.

When Joseph saw them, however, he almost dropped the pen and scroll he held to keep track of the accounts. He could not believe that after so many years he would see his brothers again. Still, he did not tell them who he was. Instead, he accused them of being spies.

"But we are brothers! There were twelve of us, but one is dead, and the youngest is with our father," the brothers said in dismay.

"I do not believe you," Joseph said. "If you are not spies, then prove it by going home and bringing your youngest brother to me.

One of you must go and get him. The rest of you will be kept under guard until the truth of what you say can be tested."

Then he put them in prison for three days. The brothers couldn't believe what was happening to them.

On the third day Joseph said to them, "I love God, so I will spare your lives as long as you do what I say. To prove that you are honest, one of you will stay in prison, and the rest can go home to your starving family, taking the corn that you have bought. Then you must bring your youngest brother to me."

The brothers stood with their mouths open. "What have we done wrong?" one whispered to another. They did not think Joseph could understand them, because they spoke Hebrew and they thought he was an Egyptian.

"I'll tell you what we did wrong," Reuben said. "We should never have thrown Joseph down the well. And you should never have sold him as a slave." The brothers knew Reuben was right. They could still remember Joseph begging them to let him go, and they had all turned away and ignored him. Now it was their turn to suffer.

When Joseph heard this he left them and began to cry, his feelings were so great. When he was able to speak again, he came back, picked out Simeon, and had him tied up in front of them.

The other ten brothers rode home. On the way they discovered their money, which Joseph had ordered to be tucked in among the grain they had bought. "Oh no," they moaned, "now it looks as though we stole the grain."

When the brothers arrived home, they told Jacob what had happened. They asked if they could take Benjamin back to Egypt.

"Absolutely not!" Jacob said. "There is no way anyone is taking my Benjamin from me. Do you see how old I am? Do you want me to die with grey hairs of worry? No. Benjamin stays here." Jacob would not listen to any more of their arguments. He thought, "It is bad enough that Joseph is dead. Now they have left Simeon behind. No, they will never take Benjamin away."

Benjamin May Go

Genesis 43.1-34

Slowly but surely the grain the brothers had brought back with them from Egypt was eaten. Soon there was hardly anything left. Jacob, his sons, their wives and their children cut back on the amount they ate each day. Soon they had hardly anything to eat. The children were so hungry that they cried. The women complained.

Again and again the brothers had asked their father to let them return to Egypt with Benjamin to buy more food. After all, Simeon was still there. But Jacob always refused. He knew it would mean letting Benjamin go.

Finally, however, he could ignore the famine no longer. He had to think about the rest of his large family. So he agreed. And Judah, the brother who had sold Joseph as a slave so long ago, said he would take special care of Benjamin. "Nothing will happen to him," he promised.

"Just to make sure," Jacob said, "take double the money. That way you can pay the Egyptian man back for what we didn't pay last time, as the money had been put back in the grain which you brought home. Take him special gifts of honey, spices, pistachio nuts, and almonds."

Jacob prayed that God would give the man in Egypt, who was actually Joseph, a good heart, and that no harm would come to Benjamin.

As soon as the brothers arrived in Egypt, they went to Joseph. When Joseph saw Benjamin with them, he told his guards to bring the brothers into his house.

The brothers thought this was very strange. Egyptians did not like to have Hebrews in their homes, and they never ate with them, either. Because it was so strange for an Egyptian to invite them into his home, the brothers were afraid they had done something wrong again.

So at the door of the house they told the servant in charge about the money they had taken home last time. "We did not know it was there until after we left," they said.

The servant told them that he had been paid for the grain, and that they were not to worry. Then he brought Simeon to them, and took the brothers into the house. When Joseph arrived, they bowed down to him and gave him their gifts.

Joseph took a good look at Benjamin. He had grown into a tall, handsome young man.

"How is your father?" Joseph asked.

"He is alive and well," the brothers answered.

Joseph looked at Benjamin again. He reached out a hand and put it on the boy's head. "May God be good to you, my son," he said. Suddenly he turned away. He felt such tender feelings for his brothers that he was about to break down and cry. So he got up and ran from the room. Once alone, he cried and cried, so great were his feelings for his brothers.

Joseph wiped away his tears and returned to the brothers. "Come," he said to them, "and we will have a big meal together."

To the brothers' amazement, Joseph seated them in order of their age, from the eldest to the youngest, and he served them from his own table. It was a grand party and lasted most of the night. But not once did Joseph tell the brothers who he really was.

The Stolen Cup

Genesis 44.1–34

The next morning the brothers rode off for home. They were happy. They had rescued Simeon, bought food for their families, and eaten with an important man. Best of all, Benjamin was safe and they did not have to worry about hurting their father again.

But Joseph had a plan. Before they left, he had ordered one of his servants to hide his favourite silver cup in Benjamin's bag. The servant in charge of Joseph's house was chasing them because the cup was missing.

He galloped alongside the brothers. "Stop your donkeys," he ordered them.

"What have we done wrong?" Reuben asked.

"One of you has stolen my master's silver cup," the servant said.

"But why would we steal?" the brothers protested. "We will make an agreement with you. If you find that cup, which you won't, then the person with whom you find it will stay in Egypt and become a slave."

The brothers were quite sure that the servant had made a big mistake. But all the same, they felt nervous.

The servant went down the line, from one to another, finally ending up at Benjamin's donkey. When he reached into Benjamin's sack, a shout went up and the servant raised the silver cup into the air.

The brothers groaned. "Oh, no! This is terrible. Benjamin what have you done?"

Benjamin was so shocked, he just shook his head. "I did not do this."

"What will we do?" the brothers cried, throwing their hands in the air. "This is the worst thing that could have happened. We cannot go home without Benjamin. Our father will die of a broken heart." The brothers cried and tore their clothes because they felt so terrible about it all.

The servant ordered them back to Joseph's palace. When they saw Joseph they ran to him and said, "We never intended to take your silver cup and we are sorry."

"You may go," Joseph said. "Only the one in whose sack the cup was found must stay behind."

"Oh, but you don't understand," the brothers cried out.

"What don't I understand?" Joseph asked.

"It is such a long story, and it is very sad," Judah said. "Our father will die if we do not bring his youngest son back to him. He has already lost one son, and he could not bear to lose this one, too.

"Please, I beg of you, let me stay here in his place. If Benjamin stays here, none of us will have lives worth living." Judah fell to his knees and begged Joseph to let Benjamin go.

The Truth Comes Out

Genesis 45.1–24

When Joseph saw Judah on his knees pleading with him, and Benjamin looking so worried, he could hardly keep from crying. He cried out to his servants, "Leave us alone. I want to be alone with these men!"

The servants ran out of the room. The brothers looked at each other. What could it mean that this powerful man wanted to speak to them alone? Were they all to be killed?

Then he called them to him. "I am your brother Joseph," he said. They did not believe him. They were so terrified, they could not listen. "Open your eyes," said Joseph, coming closer to them, "I am Joseph, the one you sold into Egypt!"

When Joseph said that, the brothers took a good look, then became even more afraid. If this powerful man really was Joseph, then he had every reason to kill them for what they had done to him.

"No, no, do not be afraid any more, brothers. Do not be angry with yourselves for making me come here, because God sent me ahead of you to save lives. For two years now there has been no food in the land, and for the next five years it will get even worse. But God sent me here to make sure there would be enough food."

Joseph's brothers stared at him with big eyes.

"Don't you see?" he said. "You did not send me here, God did. God made me ruler of all Egypt, over everyone but Pharaoh. This was all part of God's plan for taking care of our family. Now hurry back to my father and tell him all these things. Tell him to bring our whole family to Egypt, and to hurry. You can all live in a part of Egypt called Goshen. I will make sure you have enough food to eat. If you don't do this, all our family will die of hunger."

Joseph threw his arms around Benjamin, gave him a big hug and started crying. He was so happy to see him again. He and his brothers spent a lot of time talking about all that had happened to them during the past years.

When Pharaoh heard the news that Joseph's brothers were in the palace, he ordered his servants to give them many wagons so that they could bring their wives, children, and possessions back to Egypt. Pharaoh was happy that Joseph's family would soon join him.

Before they left, Joseph gave the brothers many animals and other beautiful gifts for his father.

"Do not quarrel along the way," he told them as they set off for home.

A NEW HOME AND A NEW BEGINNING

All Together Again

Genesis 45.25–46.29

When the brothers arrived home, they told Jacob that Joseph was alive and that he was a ruler in Egypt.

At first Jacob did not believe them. He was stunned. When he heard the whole story, however, and saw all the beautiful gifts, he became a completely different man. "Oh yes! I believe you! My son Joseph is still alive. I will go and see him before I die."

All of Jacob's family, his sons and their wives, children, servants, and animals made the long trip out to Egypt. What a sight they were, with the women and children all riding in the wagons Pharaoh had given them.

On the way, Jacob stopped to pray to God and thank him for watching over his family. That night God spoke to Jacob in a vision. "Jacob! Jacob!" God said.

"Here I am," he said.

"I am God, the God of your father. Do not be afraid to move to Egypt, for I will make you into a great nation there. I will be with you and make sure your family returns to this land I have promised you. And Jacob, you will see Joseph again before you die."

Jacob and his family went to Egypt. When they got there, they were met by Joseph in his chariot. As soon as Joseph saw Jacob, he leapt out of his chariot, ran over to his father and threw his arms around him. The two men wept for happiness. They had been apart for so long, and they loved each other very much.

The Nation of Israel Settles In Egypt

Genesis 46.30–50.26

Joseph brought his whole family to meet Pharaoh. He asked permission for them to live in the land of Goshen. It was very beautiful there. Joseph made sure that his brothers, their wives, and their children had enough food to eat.

Jacob's people, the Israelites, bought land and worked hard.

One day Jacob called for Joseph and made him swear that when he died, Joseph would bury Jacob back in the land of Canaan, where Abraham and Isaac were also buried. Joseph agreed. When Jacob had finished speaking to his sons, he lay back in bed and died. He had lived a long, full life and it was time for him to die.

Joseph went to Pharaoh and asked for permission to bury his father in Canaan. Pharaoh agreed.

So a huge crowd of people – Joseph, his brothers, and many Egyptian servants, made the long journey back to Canaan. Jacob was buried in the same cave as his father and mother. And Joseph and his brothers wept and were sad for many days afterwards.

When the family returned to Egypt, the brothers became afraid. With their father gone, Joseph might decide to hurt them in return for the way they had hurt him when they threw him down the well and sold him as a slave. So they went to Joseph and begged his forgiveness. They were afraid of Joseph, because he was so powerful.

Joseph said to them, "God has turned the bad into good. Do not be afraid of me, we are brothers." He was kind to his brothers and their families, making sure they always had enough to eat.

Joseph and all his brothers and their families stayed in Egypt during the rest of the famine and for many years afterwards. Joseph lived to be an old man. Not only did he have grandsons, but he lived long enough to see his great-grandsons.

Before Joseph died, he made his brothers promise that one day the family would return to the land God had given them, in Canaan. He asked that when they did, they would take his bones back there, so he could be buried next to his father.

THE BABY WHOSE CRYING WAS HEARD BY A PRINCESS

Unrest In Egypt

Exodus 1.1-22

Nearly four hundred years later there was a very cruel Pharaoh in Egypt who made the Israelites — who were also called the Hebrews — work for him as slaves. Again and again the Israelites cried out to God, "Save us, Lord! We have lived in this land for too long. Please take us away from here soon." They prayed and prayed. But there were cruel men who whipped them and made them work harder until the old and weak died. The harder they were whipped, the more the Israelites complained. This was a very sad time for the people of Israel.

But despite all the hard work Pharaoh ordered the Israelites to do, their families continued to grow. Pharaoh was afraid of all the Israelites and did not want their boys to grow into men. He called the two midwives, who helped Israelite women have their babies.

"When you are helping the Hebrew women give birth," he ordered them, "check to see if the baby is a boy. If it is, kill him, but let the girls live."

The midwives, who were like nurses, listened to Pharaoh and trembled. They knew Pharaoh could kill them if they did not do what he told them. But there was someone else they feared even more, and that was God. It was wrong to kill babies, they knew that. They prayed to God for the strength to do what was right, no matter what Pharaoh wanted.

The midwives chose not to kill the Israelite baby boys. When Pharaoh heard the news, he sent for them again. "Why didn't you do as you were told?" he roared.

The women were scared, but they wanted to protect the babies. They said, "Hebrew women are different from Egyptian women. They do not need us to help as much. Their babies are born so fast, we are never there on time."

God blessed the two women for protecting the babies of his people. He stopped Pharaoh from punishing them. He gave the two midwives loving husbands, and children of their own.

Pharaoh, however, was still not happy. He ordered all his people, the Egyptians, to kill every Hebrew baby boy they could find.

"Throw their sons into the River Nile!" he said. "But the daughters may live."

A Baby In a Boat

Exodus 2.1-4

Pharaoh's order to kill all the Israelite baby boys struck terror into the hearts of Hebrew parents. They loved their children more than their own lives. "What can we do?" they cried out to each other.

Time and time again, as soon as an Israelite mother gave birth to a little boy, the soldiers found out and came to her house. Despite the mother's screams, they would take the little boy from her. She knew she would never see her son again.

One mother who had given birth to a little boy tried everything she could think of to keep her boy alive. She was desperate to save him.

For three months she managed to keep the baby hidden. He hardly ever cried, and none of the soldiers passing by her home ever heard him. When he was three months old, however, she could hide him no longer.

"There must be something we can do," she would cry to her husband every night. Night after night they prayed about it. Their little girl, Miriam, the boy's elder sister, prayed with them. Then the family had an idea. The mother wove a basket out of reeds, and then covered it with tar. The basket became a little boat. Then they took the baby, and wrapped him in soft blankets, and laid him in the basket.

Miriam and her mother brought the basket down to the river and gently placed it in the tall grass at the edge of the river. "Watch him, Miriam," the mother said. "I must go home or the soldiers will wonder what I am doing. They have not stopped watching me ever since I told them that the baby I carried was already dead. I will go home and pray. But you watch the basket, and run and tell me as soon as anything happens."

The little boy in the basket was sound asleep. The waves gently rocked him, just as his mother did whenever she wanted him to sleep. And Miriam watched.

Saved By a Princess

Exodus 2.5-9

God had heard the prayers of the baby boy's parents and sister. He had special plans for that baby. As the basket floated in the river, one of Pharaoh's daughters, a princess, chose that moment to bathe in the river.

Suddenly the princess saw the basket. "Look over there," she said to one of her servants. "I wonder if there is anything in that basket? Go and get it." The servant took the basket to the princess, who opened it.

There, inside the basket, was a beautiful baby with tiny fingers. "Oh, look at him," the princess said. She scooped up the baby and cuddled him.

"Who would want to lose such a handsome boy as this?" the servants said.

"He must be a Hebrew boy," the princess answered, for she knew the order her father had sent throughout the land. She felt sorry for the baby. "He is so hungry – how can we feed him?" she asked.

Meanwhile, Miriam had been watching closely, praying that the princess would want to save her little brother. Miriam ran up to the princess. Out of breath, she said, "I know a Hebrew woman who could feed him. Shall I go and get her?"

"Please do," said the princess. So Miriam went and brought their own mother.

The princess asked the woman to feed the baby with her own milk. She even paid her for doing it! She handed the baby back to his mother. "If the soldiers bother you, just tell them that the baby is in my care," the princess said. The family were overjoyed with what had happened, and thanked God for looking after them so well.

Moses Strikes a Blow For Freedom

Exodus 2.11–14

Later, when the child was old enough, his mother took him back to Pharaoh's daughter, who adopted him as her own son. "I will call him Moses," she said, "since I pulled him out of the water."

As Moses grew older, the princess made sure he learned his lessons. She ordered the wise men to teach Moses how to think and ask questions. He learned the histories of Egypt and all the peoples who lived there. Moses knew he was a Hebrew, and as he learned about Abraham, Isaac, and Jacob, he felt glad he was a member of God's chosen people.

Whenever he rode through the streets, however, and saw how roughly the Israelites were treated, he was angry.

"It's not fair," he cried to his mother, the princess.

The princess looked at her boy. She felt that one day he would be a great man and he deserved the truth, but all she could say was, "We cannot question what Pharaoh does. He is the king."

The years went by, and Moses grew into a man. One day, Moses was walking in the streets when he saw an Egyptian beating to death a Hebrew slave. Moses felt anger burn in him like a fire.

"No!" he yelled, and rushed at the Egyptian, killing him. He hid the Egyptian's body in the sand.

Moses knew it was a terrible thing to kill. If he were caught for killing an Egyptian, even his mother the princess could not save him. But he did not think anyone had seen him.

The next day Moses saw two Hebrews fighting. "Don't," he said to them. "Isn't it bad enough that the Egyptians fight you? Save your strength for them."

The Hebrews looked at Moses' fine clothes. They laughed at him. "Who are you to tell us not to fight? Didn't you kill an Egyptian yesterday?" They laughed because they knew that as soon as Pharaoh heard what Moses had done, Moses would be in trouble.

Moses grew afraid. "If these two Hebrews know what I have done, who else might know?" he wondered. "I must leave Egypt, and quickly!"

Moses Becomes a Shepherd

Exodus 2.15-25

Pharaoh did find out about Moses killing the Egyptian, and he sent guards to catch Moses. Moses ran away from Egypt and went to live in the land of Midian. He wandered a long way until he was sure Pharaoh's men had lost him. Finally he saw a well and went to rest beside it.

Soon seven girls came to the well to collect water for their sheep. They were daughters of a priest who lived nearby. As the girls gave water to their sheep, some other shepherds came along and pushed the girls away from the well.

Moses came to their rescue and told the shepherds to leave the girls alone. Then he helped them by giving water to their flock himself.

The girls ran home and told their father, called Jethro, that an Egyptian had helped them. Their father sent them to get Moses.

He told his daughters, "Let us show our thanks to this stranger. Invite him to come here and eat with us."

Moses agreed to stay with Jethro, and after some time the priest gave Moses his daughter Zipporah, to be his wife.

Some time later, Moses and Zipporah had a son and Moses named him Gershom, which means "A Foreigner There." Moses said, "I am an alien in a foreign land."

Moses stayed in the desert with the Midianites for a long time, bringing up his family. He had many children and grandchildren. He learnt many things from Jethro.

One of the most important lessons Jethro taught Moses was where to find food and water in the desert, how to know when to stop and rest, and how to make the desert a friend, instead of an enemy. God knew all these things would be very useful to Moses one day, and God was preparing him for that time.

While Moses lived with the Midianites, the cruel Pharaoh died. The next Pharaoh, however, was no better and the Israelites continued to work as slaves, groaning under the heavy load of work they always had to do.

Again and again they cried out to God. God heard their cry and remembered his promise to Abraham, Isaac, and Jacob. God had a plan for his people.

GOD CALLS MOSES
The Burning Bush

Exodus 3.1–10

One day Moses was out in the desert looking after Jethro's sheep, when he saw a very strange sight. At the foot of a mountain he saw a bush on fire. But the fire did not spread, and the bush did not look black, nor did it burn away. Moses climbed up some rocks to get a better look.

As he got closer to the bush, he heard a voice say, "Moses, Moses!"

"Here I am," said Moses.

"Do not come any closer," the voice said. "Take off your sandals, for you are standing on holy ground. I am the God of your father, the God of Abraham, the God of Isaac, and the God of Jacob."

When Moses heard this, he fell to the ground and covered his face. He was afraid to look at God.

The Lord said, "I have seen how unhappy my people are in Egypt. I have seen how cruelly the Egyptians treat them. The time has come for me to rescue them and bring them back to the land I promised so long ago to Abraham and Isaac. It is a spacious, rich and fertile land, where there is plenty of water and crops grow easily.

"Go now, Moses. I am sending you to Pharaoh to lead my people, the Israelites, out of Egypt."

Moses thought to himself, "How can God talk to me?" He was very scared of the power God had. When he heard God say that he, Moses, would be the one to lead the Israelites out of Egypt, he trembled even more.

A Hundred and One Excuses

Exodus 3.11–4.9

Moses said, "Who am I, that I should go to Pharaoh and bring the Israelites out of Egypt?"

"How can I possibly convince Pharaoh to let all his slaves go free?" Moses thought. He knew that he had no special talents.

God's answer to Moses was simple — "I will be with you."

Moses said, "But no one will believe that I speak for you. How will I explain to the people who you are?"

God said to Moses, "I am who I am. That is my name. Tell the people I am the God of Abraham, the God of Isaac, and the God of Jacob. Tell them the God who chose them as a special people has sent you."

Moses was still not ready to do what God asked him. He did not want to go on this mission at all. He even dared to make God angry by coming up with excuse after excuse. Moses said, "When I tell them who you are, they will not believe me."

"Just to prove that I am with you," God said, "ask Pharaoh if you may take the people on a three-day journey into the desert. Ask Pharaoh for just three days when the people can hold a religious festival in my name. I know that Pharaoh will refuse; but I can work miracles and strike down the Egyptians. I will even make the Egyptian people want to give you gifts when you leave Egypt."

Moses said, "But what if they still do not listen to me?"

The Lord asked, "What is that in your hand?"

"A stick," Moses answered.

"Throw it on the ground," God said. When Moses did so, the stick became a snake and Moses ran from it. When God told him to pick it up again, Moses reached out and picked up the snake. Instantly, it became his shepherd's stick again.

God gave Moses two more special signs for the people. First, when Moses put his hand inside his robe, then took it out, the skin looked dry and dead, white as snow. But when Moses put his hand back in his robe and took it out again, the skin was all better. And if Moses took water out of the River Nile and spilt it on the ground, the water would become blood. These would be signs to the people that Moses spoke God's words.

A Spokesman For Moses

Exodus 4.10-16

Despite all the promises and signs God gave Moses to help the people believe him, Moses kept arguing with God. God had promised Moses he would work miracles and make Pharaoh let the people go. This was still not good enough for Moses. He was very stubborn and really did not want to do the job.

Moses made one last excuse. "Lord, I cannot speak well. People will not understand me, and Pharaoh will laugh. He will not bother listening to me."

The Lord said, "Who made your mouth? I did. I will help you speak when the time comes."

Moses begged God to send someone else. This made God angry. He had chosen Moses to do a great thing, and promised he would be with Moses every step of the way. God grew tired of hearing all Moses' excuses.

"Your brother Aaron may speak for you," God said. "It will be as if he were your mouth. I will help both of you speak and will teach you what to do."

26

Moses had run out of excuses. He bowed his head, still shaking from having dared to argue with God. He was God's chosen man. But he felt very small when he thought that God would walk with him on this mission.

Moses was just starting to learn to trust God and obey him.

MOSES AGAINST PHARAOH
Pharaoh Says "No"

Exodus 4.17–5.21

Moses took his stick in his hand, said "good-bye" to his father-in-law, and started on his journey back to Egypt. On the way Moses met his elder brother, Aaron. God had told Aaron to go out into the desert and meet Moses. Moses was especially glad to see Aaron, because God had said Aaron would do the talking for him.

When Moses and Aaron arrived in Egypt, they went straight to the Israelite leaders. They showed them God's signs and told them what God had said. When the people heard that the Lord was concerned about their suffering, and had heard their groans, they bowed down and thanked God, praising him.

Next, Moses and Aaron went to Pharaoh. They said, "The Lord, the God of Israel says, 'Let my people go, so that they can hold a religious festival, and worship me for three days.' "

Pharaoh said, "Who is the Lord, that I should obey him? I do not know this Lord, and I will not let the people of Israel go."

Moses and Aaron asked Pharaoh a second time, but again he refused. This time, though, he grew angry. He had thought the Israelites were working too hard to have time for their religion.

Pharaoh ordered the slave drivers to punish the Israelites. "They must make and carry just as many bricks as before, but now they must find the straw for the bricks themselves," he said.

The Israelites made bricks from mud and straw. If the mud dried without straw in it, it was not strong, and crumbled into dust. Before Pharaoh's order, the slaves would get the straw from the slave drivers.

A few of the slave drivers were Israelites. They went to Pharaoh and complained, "The work is too much. No matter how much the people are whipped, they can never find the straw and make the same number of bricks as before."

"Lazy! Lazy! That's what you are!" Pharaoh shouted at them. "That is why Moses is wanting you to take three days off for some religious holiday."

When the Israelite slave drivers left Pharaoh and saw Aaron and Moses, they told them angrily, "See what you have done! You have made the work-load our people must bear even heavier. You are no help at all!"

God Promises Action

Exodus 5.22–7.16

Moses prayed to the Lord and said, "God, I am so confused. What is happening? You brought me here to rescue your people, but now they must work even harder than before. What should I do?"

God said, "I am the Lord and I will bring you out from Egypt. Israel is like a favourite child to me, like my first child. Because Pharaoh will not let you go, I will do great things. I will kill the Egyptians' eldest sons, because they have threatened my chosen people. There will be no doubt among the Egyptians or the Israelites that I was the one who rescued them. They will know that I am God."

When Moses first went to Pharaoh, Pharaoh had said that he did not know the Lord. Soon, though, he would know without a doubt who God was. It was all part of God's plan.

God told Moses, "Go back to Pharaoh and ask him a third time to let my people go."

Moses did not want to. "I have caused so much trouble already," he thought. "Look how much worse off the Israelites have been since I bothered Pharaoh. What if it becomes even worse if I ask again?"

Moses swallowed hard and argued with God. "Why should Pharaoh listen to me?" he asked.

The Lord reminded Moses that he would not have to do the talking. Aaron could speak for him. He warned Moses that when Pharaoh did not listen, he, the Lord, would act.

Moses and Aaron went to Pharaoh a third time. To prove they really spoke for God, they threw Moses' stick on to the ground and it became a snake. Pharaoh called his magicians and when they threw their magic sticks down they became snakes, too, but Moses' snake ate theirs. Still, Pharaoh would not do as Moses asked. The Lord told Moses that because Pharaoh would not listen, the time had come for God to show Pharaoh his power.

Terrible Plagues

Exodus 7.17–10.29

Pharaoh refused to let God's people go, so God punished the Egyptians.

He sent ten plagues to Egypt. Plagues are bad events in nature which happen to a large area all at once. Pharaoh sent for his magicians and wise men to make the plagues go away, but God showed that he was in control by ending the plagues only when Moses asked the Lord to stop them.

During the first plague, water turned to blood. When Moses stretched his stick over the River Nile, it turned into a river of blood. All the streams and canals, ponds and puddles, filled with blood instead of water. The fish died, and the river stank.

A week later God told Moses to go to Pharaoh again and ask him to let the Israelites go. He told Moses to warn Pharaoh that if he did not obey, God would fill the Nile with frogs.

When Pharaoh refused, the frogs came in thousands. They climbed out of the river, the streams, and the canals, and covered the land of Egypt. They even went into the houses. People woke up in the morning to the sound of frogs croaking right in their ears.

Pharaoh asked Moses to make the frogs go away. So Moses prayed, and the frogs all died. But Pharaoh still did not believe in God. He still would not let God's people go.

Then God sent gnats, tiny flies that bite, to Egypt. They were everywhere. The Egyptians had to cover their mouths whenever they talked, otherwise the little flies got caught in their throats.

Then God sent a plague of bigger flies.

God sent diseases which made the cattle ill, and the skin on people and animals turn red and itch.

God sent hail and thunderstorms. The wind blew hard, and insects called locusts came in huge clouds, eating every green leaf they found. Soon there was nothing left in all the land, only bare branches and twigs.

Lastly, God caused the light of the sun to go out for three days. Instead of night turning into day, it was always dark, with no sunshine.

God gave Pharaoh chance after chance, but he would not change his mind. He still would not let the Israelites go. In fact, after God made the sun go dark, Pharaoh was so angry, he yelled at Moses, "Get out of my sight!"

Moses, who was angry because Pharaoh had hurt the people over and over again, replied, "I will never appear before you again."

The Last Plague

Exodus 11.1-10

Moses looked at Pharaoh that one last time. He was furious. "How can this man be so blind?" Moses wondered. God had performed miracle after miracle through Moses. Pharaoh had refused to listen, refused to obey. He was worse than blind. The blind do not choose to be blind. But over and over again Pharaoh chose not to believe what God had shown him. He would not believe in God and his power.

God warned Pharaoh through Moses that he would send one more plague, the tenth. After this one, Pharaoh would let the Israelites leave Egypt.

Moses told Pharaoh, "The eldest son of all Egyptian families, whether free or slave, will die, as will the first-born of all your cattle. The children of the Israelite families, however, will be safe. This is to show you God's power, and to let you know that he sees a difference between your people and his."

Pharaoh did not believe such a thing could ever happen. It would mean that his eldest son would die, as would the eldest child of every Egyptian family in the entire land. They would lose all the new calves and goats and sheep, too. Pharaoh trembled with rage that anyone would dare to threaten him in this way.

If he had stopped to think, and remembered how the plagues had all gone away whenever Moses prayed to God to stop them, he might have realized that God did not have to kill all those children. All Pharaoh had to do was to let the Israelites go.

But Pharaoh would not believe in God's power. He closed his mind and told himself, "This can never happen."

"Out! Out of here!" he yelled at Moses.

Moses left Pharaoh, and the two men never saw each other again.

Adventure Story Bible   Old Testament

New Testament